47 RONIN
A Samurai Story from Japan

The story of the forty-seven ronin is a very famous one in Japan. It is a true story about real people, but many of the facts are now lost in time. Soon after the ronin took their revenge, the story was retold in plays, known as *Chushingura*. Since then the story has been retold in song, story, drama, television plays, visual art, and many films. Each time the story is retold, the details change. But one thing does not change – this story is still as famous in Japan today as it was 300 years ago.

The story begins in Edo (now modern Tokyo) in spring 1701, in the Shogun's palace. Lord Asano is taking lessons in palace ceremony from Lord Kira, one of the lords in the Shogun's palace. Kira has only hard words for Asano, and by the end of that terrible day, Lord Asano is dead. Asano's samurai are now *ronin* – samurai without a lord or master. They have no home, no place in the world. They have only loyalty to their dead lord.

This is the true story of the forty-seven ronin . . .

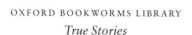

OXFORD BOOKWORMS LIBRARY
True Stories

47 Ronin

A Samurai Story from Japan

Stage 1 (400 headwords)

Series Editor: Jennifer Bassett
Founder Editor: Tricia Hedge
Activities Editors: Jennifer Bassett and Christine Lindop

NOTES ABOUT SAMURAI

Samurai

Warriors, famous fighting men in the old days in Japan. They lived by a special set of rules, the samurai code of honour (*bushido* in Japanese).

Ronin

Samurai without a *daimyo* (a lord or master). In Japan today ronin are more often called *roshi*.

Seppuku

Ritual suicide – killing yourself by cutting your stomach open with a knife. This was part of *bushido*, the samurai code of honour, and for samurai, it was better to commit *seppuku* than to live a life without honour.

Daimyo

A lord, a powerful ruler of a region in Japan in the old days. *Daimyo* often had their own armies of three or four hundred samurai to guard their castles and land.

Shogun

The military ruler of Japan in the old days, under the Emperor.

JENNIFER BASSETT

47 Ronin

A Samurai Story from Japan

Illustrated by
Dragon76

OXFORD UNIVERSITY PRESS

OXFORD
UNIVERSITY PRESS

Great Clarendon Street, Oxford, OX2 6DP, United Kingdom

Oxford University Press is a department of the University of Oxford.
It furthers the University's objective of excellence in research, scholarship,
and education by publishing worldwide. Oxford is a registered trade
mark of Oxford University Press in the UK and in certain other countries

© Oxford University Press 2014

The moral rights of the author have been asserted

First published in Oxford Bookworms 2014

10 9 8 7 6 5

ISBN: 978 0 19 478612 6

A complete recording of this Bookworms edition of
47 Ronin: A Samurai Story from Japan is available.

Printed in China

Word count (main text): 6,079 words

For more information on the Oxford Bookworms Library,
visit www.oup.com/elt/gradedreaders

ACKNOWLEDGEMENTS

Illustrations by: Dragon 76/Dutch Uncle Agency

The publishers would like to thank the following for their permission to reproduce photographs:
Alamy Images p.42 (Grave of Asano Naganori at Sengaku-ji temple/pf); Getty Images p.1
(Three samurai warriors in armour, circa 1880/Kusakabe Kimbei/Hulton Archive).

CONTENTS

PEOPLE IN THIS STORY

In the old days, important men in Japan were often called by their court titles, not by their real names. In this story real names are used.

Lord Kira Yoshinaka, *a lord in the Shogun's palace*
  (court title: Kira Kozuke-no-suke Yoshinaka)
Lord Asano Naganori, *the daimyo of Ako Castle*
  (court title: Asano Takumi-no-kami Naganori)
Oishi Yoshio, *captain of Lord Asano's samurai*
  (court title: Oishi Kura-no-suke Yoshio)

Daigaku, *Lord Asano's younger brother*
Chikara, *Oishi's son*
Riku, *Oishi's wife*

Hayami }	
Kataoka }	
Hara }	
Mimura }	
Horibe }	*Ten of Lord Asano's samurai (later, ronin)*
Okuda }	
Yoshida }	
Isogai }	
Terasaka }	
Hazama }	

Samurai

In the old days in Japan, the samurai were warriors, fighting men. They served a *daimyo*, one of the great Japanese lords. They lived in his castle, fought for him, and died for him. They fought with long swords and short swords, spears, and bows and arrows. They were brave, fierce men, famous for their loyalty to their lord.

CHAPTER 1

The death of Asano

'Good morning, Lord Asano.'

The speaker was Lord Kira Yoshinaka, a tall man, in black. He stood in the middle of a room in the Shogun's palace. He watched Lord Asano, and waited.

Lord Asano Naganori was a younger man, thirty-four years to Lord Kira's sixty years. He walked slowly across the room from the door, and stopped in front of Kira.

'Lord Kira,' he said coldly. 'Good morning.' And then he bowed, just a small bow of the head.

Lord Kira bowed too, an even smaller bow. He smiled, but his eyes were cold.

'Are you ready for your next lesson, Lord Asano?' he said. 'You have much to learn about palace ceremony, and you are a very slow student. Shall we begin?'

Lord Asano bowed again, but did not speak. His mouth was a thin, hard line. Every day Kira called him 'slow', or 'stupid', or 'difficult', and he did not like it.

In the Shogun's palace at Edo in the year 1701, ceremony was very important. The right words, at the right time of day. The right bow, small or deep, for different people. The right clothes, at different hours of the day. The right presents, for the right people . . . This was the way of life in the Shogun's palace, and Lord Kira was the teacher of ceremony – for this Shogun, and for

Lord Kira bowed too, an even smaller bow.

many Shoguns before him. After forty years as a teacher, Kira knew everything about the ceremony of the palace.

But Lord Asano knew nothing. He was a *daimyo* from the country, from Ako Castle, a place seventeen days' journey by horse to the south-west of Edo. The *daimyo* were powerful men in Japan at this time, and were rulers in their own part of the country. But *daimyo* must also serve the Shogun, and every year the Shogun called two of them to his palace at Edo.

'Every day is the same,' said Asano angrily, at his house in Edo that evening. 'Every day I must do *this* ceremony, or *that* ceremony, I must stand *here*, or *there*, bow to *this* person, or *that* person. And I must do six months of this! Every day Kira calls me bad names! I make mistakes because *he* is a bad teacher!'

Hayami, one of Asano's samurai, helped him with his ceremonial clothes. Hayami was very good with the bow and arrow, but not so good with words.

'Lord, I heard something about Kira,' he said.

'What?' said Asano.

'He likes presents, and money. The other *daimyo* gives him presents or money, and then Kira is happy, and the lessons go well. Why don't you give him a present?'

'No!' shouted Asano. 'I am Lord Asano of Ako, and I do not give presents to the Shogun's servants! His job is to teach me ceremony, not to ask for presents!'

Hayami said nothing more, but he was afraid for his

master. Every day Asano came back from the palace with an angry face, and angry words.

'How is this going to end?' Hayami said to Kataoka, another of Asano's samurai. 'Four more months of this. What can I do? We need Oishi here. Lord Asano doesn't listen to me, but he listens to Oishi sometimes.'

Every day Asano came back from the palace with an angry face.

But Oishi Yoshio was at Ako Castle, a long way away. He was the captain of Lord Asano's three hundred samurai. When Lord Asano came to Edo, most of his samurai came with him, but Oishi stayed behind at Ako to take care of everything there.

It ended suddenly on a spring day in 1701.

The day began well, with a blue sky and the song of birds in the palace gardens. Lord Asano arrived at the palace, put on his ceremonial clothes, and went for his lesson with Lord Kira.

Perhaps Kira was tired that day. Perhaps he was angry because there were no presents from Lord Asano. Perhaps he just did not like the young lord from Ako.

'You must wait,' he told Asano. 'I have another, more important meeting first.' He turned his back on Lord Asano. 'What a stupid man!' Kira said. Usually, he said things like this in a quiet voice, but today he did not speak quietly, and everybody in the great palace room could hear him. 'I hear Asano's wife is stupid too, and his children,' Lord Kira said to the room.

Something broke inside Lord Asano. 'Lord Kira, stop a moment,' he cried.

'Well, what is it?' said Kira, turning back to Asano.

People remembered this moment for many years. Asano drew his sword, and attacked Lord Kira. With a cry, Kira put his hand to his head, but he did not fall.

Asano drew his sword, and attacked Lord Kira.

Asano lifted his sword again, but now there were palace guards around him. They pulled him to the floor, and held his sword arm. Lord Kira ran away. There was a deep cut on his face.

The Shogun's palace was a place of ceremony, not a place for fighting. It was a terrible thing to do – to draw a sword and attack someone inside the palace.

The attack happened at about midday. At one o'clock the guards took Asano to the house of another *daimyo*. At four o'clock an order came from the Shogun. 'Lord Asano must die, but because he is a *daimyo*, he can die the samurai way, with honour. He can commit *seppuku*.'

And so it happened. At six o'clock that same day Lord Asano of Ako committed *seppuku*. He took out his long knife, and cut into his stomach from left to right.

Outside the palace Lord Asano's samurai, Kataoka, knew nothing of this. He waited for his master to leave the palace at the end of the day, but Asano never came. At last another *daimyo* told Kataoka the terrible news.

Kataoka ran back to Asano's house in Edo, and called for Hayami and the other samurai. 'Our lord is dead,' he cried. 'Get the horses ready! We must ride to Ako at once!'

CHAPTER 2
The plan

At that time, it was usually a journey of seventeen days from Edo to Ako, but Kataoka and Hayami did the journey in ten days. When they arrived at Ako Castle, they were tired, dirty, hungry, and thirsty.

Kataoka and Hayami were tired, dirty, hungry, and thirsty.

Oishi Yoshio, the captain of the Ako samurai, was not pleased with them. 'Look at you!' he said. 'What kind of samurai are you? Dirty clothes, dirty horses . . .'

But Oishi forgot about that when he heard the terrible news of Lord Asano's death.

'And that's not all,' said Hayami. He pushed the hair out of his eyes. 'The Shogun's government is going to take Lord Asano's castle, his land, his money – everything! Can they do that, Oishi?'

'They're taking Lord Asano's body to the temple of Sengaku-ji.'

'Yes,' said Oishi. 'They can. To draw a sword in the Shogun's palace is a crime. But why did Lord Asano attack Kira? What happened? Did they fight?'

'We don't know,' said Kataoka, 'we weren't there! But Lord Asano was angry every day because of Lord Kira.'

'But Asano didn't kill Kira?' said Oishi.

'No,' said Hayami. 'Kira is alive and well. People say that he just has a cut on his head.'

'And where is Lord Asano's body now?' asked Oishi.

'They're taking it to the temple of Sengaku-ji,' said Kataoka, 'just outside Edo. Some of our samurai went with the body. Then they are coming back to Ako.'

During the next days, Lord Asano's samurai made the journey down to Ako. Some of them brought news.

'Lord Asano's younger brother, Daigaku, is under house arrest in Edo,' Yoshida told Oishi. Yoshida was one of the older samurai. He and Oishi were old friends.

'Did you see Daigaku?' asked Oishi.

'Yes, just for two minutes. They're going to send him away, to Hiroshima, to the Asano family there.'

Soon there were nearly three hundred of Asano's samurai at Ako, and Oishi Yoshio called a meeting. It was a noisy, angry meeting.

Horibe was a famous swordsman. He was a fierce fighter, and a brave man, but he did not often stop to think before he spoke. He was the first to speak.

'Lord Asano is dead because of Kira,' he shouted to the meeting. 'Kira is a killer. A man cannot live under the same sky as the killer of his lord. This is the code of the samurai! When do we attack Kira?'

The samurai began to talk, but Oishi held up his hand. 'Nobody questions your honour as a samurai, Horibe. But we are not samurai now, we are ronin. We have no master, no lord. The Shogun's government killed Lord Asano because of a crime – the crime of drawing a sword in the palace. And why did this crime happen? Because of Lord Kira. We want revenge for our lord's death, and that means Kira must die. But he knows that, and he has many friends in the government. So we must be careful, we must be clever.'

'Careful? Clever?' shouted Horibe. 'What kind of samurai are you? We must attack Lord Kira at once! In Edo, people in the streets are saying that. They know we must take revenge for Asano's death. People *want* us to do that! It is the samurai way!'

'So you want to die a dog's death outside the palace?' called Yoshida. 'How many guards are there at the palace? Eh? Tell me that! Hundreds! We can't get near Kira – he knows we want him, so he has hundreds of guards around him, day and night.'

'The government is going to take Ako Castle away from the Asano family,' called another samurai. 'When the government soldiers come here, can we fight them?

'A man cannot live under the same sky as the killer of his lord.'

Can we hold Ako Castle for Daigaku? He's the head of the Asano family now.'

Kataoka answered this question. 'For a week, perhaps. But not longer. No, the Asano family at Ako is finished. We must leave Ako Castle and begin new lives as ronin.'

'So what can we do?' called Okuda, one of Horibe's friends. 'Tell us, Oishi! What can we do?'

'What do you want?' said Oishi. 'Do you want revenge? Revenge has a price, and the price is death. We cannot hope to live after we take our revenge on Kira. We must commit *seppuku* – everyone of us.'

'We are samurai!' cried a man called Hara. 'Death with

'We can wait a long, long time for revenge.'

honour is always better than a life without honour. That is the samurai code!'

Oishi smiled. 'There are brave hearts in this room. Now go away, and think. Think about the samurai way. Where is the road to honour? Can you live under the same sky as the killer of your *daimyo*? Think long and carefully. Talk to your families, and come back here in three days. Or leave Ako and begin a new life.'

In the next two days many ronin left the castle. They took their families and went away, perhaps to serve a new *daimyo*, perhaps to work in the cities, perhaps to go hungry. The life of a ronin was not easy.

After three days Oishi called the next meeting. He and Yoshida stood at the door and watched. Horibe, Okuda, and their friends arrived first, of course. Then more came, twenty, thirty, forty, fifty . . . sixty-two.

Yoshida closed the doors, and Oishi began to speak.

'You are here because you want revenge for the death of our *daimyo*. You are true samurai, loyal to your lord in life – and in death. We must make a league together – a league for revenge. But for now, we must be silent, we must be secret, we must wait for months, maybe years, before we can move. We cannot attack Kira now, because he and his guards are waiting for us. But when he forgets about us, then we can move. Because we, the ronin – we do not forget. We can wait a long, long time for revenge.'

CHAPTER 3

The long wait

And so it was. The soldiers of the Shogun's government came to Ako, took the castle and the land. And then the sixty-two ronin left Ako to go their different ways. Oishi talked to every ronin in the league before they left Ako, and every man had a plan.

Some of the ronin went to Edo. There, they found jobs as workmen, guards, or gardeners. Other ronin went to live in Osaka or other cities.

'Live very quietly,' Oishi told them. 'Don't talk about revenge, don't talk about anything to anybody. Meet secretly, and be careful of spies. Kira's men are going to be everywhere, watching and listening, all the time.'

Oishi took his family, his wife and three children, to live near Kyoto. Three of the ronin went with him – Kataoka, Mimura, and Hara. Kataoka and Mimura lived in Oishi's house, and Hara found a job.

'What kind of job?' said Oishi.

Hara laughed. 'I'm teaching boys how to shoot with bow and arrows,' he said.

'That's not a job for a samurai!' said Kataoka.

'But we're not samurai now, we're ronin, remember?' said Hara. 'And a ronin needs rice to eat.'

Weeks went past, and weeks turned into months. Oishi began to live a very different life now from his old life as captain of the Asano samurai. Every day he went into the town, to the old houses down by the river. He made new friends, and spent his time with bad people. Often, he was out all night.

Every day Oishi went into the town, to the old houses down by the river.

Kataoka and Mimura watched this, and they were not happy about it.

'Why does he go to these places?' said Mimura.

'Why don't you ask him?' Kataoka said.

'Not me!' Mimura said. 'He gets angry when you ask questions. He gets angry at bad news too. You remember when the news came about the seven ronin?'

Seven of the ronin from Ako did not want to be in the league against Kira any longer. The numbers were now down to fifty-five.

One day more news arrived – from one of the ronin in Edo. This man, Isogai, worked in the Shogun's palace gardens. He could watch government workers when they came and went, and sometimes he heard things. He sent this message to Oishi.

Lord Kira does not work in the palace now. His job is finished. People say that the Shogun is not pleased with him. Kira is living in his daimyo house, a big mansion near the Sumida river. Horibe says, can we attack him now?

Oishi suddenly came alive again. 'No, no, no! Not yet!' he said. 'I must go to Edo and talk to them. Kataoka, come with me. Mimura – stay here with my family.'

In Edo, Oishi met secretly with some of the ronin in the league. 'Listen,' he said. 'Kira's wife is from the Uesugi family, and they are very rich and powerful. There are many Uesugi guards around Kira's mansion, because he is still afraid of us. We can never get past all those guards with just fifty-five men. We must wait.'

'But how long?' said Horibe. 'Kira is an old man, and he could die any day! Where is our revenge then?'

'Begin planning,' said Oishi. 'Everybody has swords, but we need armour, spears, and bows and arrows. You can begin to find them, but secretly. And hide them well!'

Oishi and Kataoka went back to Kyoto, and again, Oishi spent his nights in the town with all kinds of bad men. People began saying that Oishi was a samurai without honour. Hara came to visit one day, and was angry.

'This is not good!' he said fiercely to Oishi. 'Where is your honour as a samurai?'

'Get out!' shouted Oishi. 'Get out of my house!'

Kataoka walked with Hara down the street.

'What's happening to him?' said Hara. 'Why is he doing this?'

'It's all right,' said Kataoka. 'Just go home, and wait.'

It was not a happy house. When he was there, Oishi shouted at everyone – his wife, his children, Kataoka, Mimura, the house servants.

Mimura often went out walking in the town, to get away from the house and all the shouting. One dark night he saw the cook from Oishi's house at a street corner, talking to two men. When they saw him, they stopped talking, and the cook walked quickly away.

Mimura crossed the street to look at the two men, but they turned away and went into a house. And in the light from the house doorway, Mimura saw something very interesting . . . He ran home at once with his news.

Mimura saw the cook from Oishi's house at a street corner.

'Oishi, I think your cook is a spy for Kira! Those men had on their coats the sign of the Uesugi family. It was very small, but I saw it clearly in the light!'

'Ha!' cried Kataoka. 'What shall we do with this spying cook, Oishi? Kill him?'

Oishi smiled. 'Nothing,' he said.

'Nothing?' said Kataoka. 'We can't do "nothing"!'

'Oh yes, we can,' said Oishi. 'This is very good. We *want* this spy to send news back to Kira – *the right kind of news*. We know the cook is a spy, but the *cook* doesn't know that *we* know. So this is good for us. He can tell Kira that I am now a samurai without honour. And who is afraid of a samurai without honour?'

'Aaah!' said Mimura. 'I think I begin to understand.'

'Good,' said Oishi. 'At last.'

Kataoka laughed.

'So,' Oishi said, 'when you talk in the house, be careful. Remember who is listening.' Suddenly, he began to shout at them. 'Get out! I'm going out into town, and nobody is going to stop me!'

Kataoka and Mimura left the room, smiling.

Time passed. Spring 1702 came, and then summer. The death of Lord Asano of Ako was now more than a year ago. In the streets of Edo, there was no talk of revenge by the Asano samurai. They were just ronin, living here and there in different cities in Japan. Their captain, Oishi

Yoshio, was without honour, and spent his time with bad men. Kira began to feel safer, and the Uesugi guards around his home went back to the Uesugi mansion across the river.

At the end of the summer Oishi came home late one night after an evening down by the river in Kyoto. When he came into the house, he shouted noisily.

'Riku! Riku! Where are you? Come here!'

Riku, his wife of twenty years, came quietly into the room, and Oishi began to shout at her.

'I'm tired of you – I don't want to see your face again. Go away! Leave my house! Go back to your father's house – our marriage is ended. I can find more beautiful girls in the town. Go!'

Riku put her face in her hands and began to cry, very quietly. From the other side of the room, Oishi shouted some more. Riku did not move.

Then she said, very quietly, 'Must I go?'

Oishi came and stood in front of her. He put his mouth close to her ear, and spoke in a whisper.

'The time is coming. I don't want you here in this house when it happens. You know why. So I must send you away, back to your father. The government cannot do anything to you when you live in your father's house. That is best for you, and the children.'

Riku looked into his face. 'Yes, I understand. Do you want me to take all the children with me?'

Oishi put his mouth close to Riku's ear, and spoke in a whisper.
'The time is coming,' he said.

They still spoke in whispers, because in that house the walls had ears.

'The younger children, yes,' said Oishi. 'But Chikara is fifteen, nearly sixteen now, and a man. He is ready to be a samurai. He can go with you, or he can stay with me. Ask him. Tell him to come and see me in the morning.'

Riku looked into his face one more time, then turned to go. Oishi put out his hand, and touched her face, just for a second. Then he, too, turned away.

That night he did not sleep. He sat for a long time in the dark, looking out at the stars in the night sky.

In the early morning his son Chikara found him there.

'Father, I want to stay here with you. I want to be a samurai, and I am ready. I am a good swordsman now.'

Oishi put his hand on his son's shoulder. 'Good man,' he said. 'The league needs strong swordsmen like you.' He was silent for a minute. 'Did you say goodbye to your mother?' he asked.

'Yes,' Chikara said. 'She left an hour ago. She . . .' He did not finish.

'Yes. I know,' said Oishi. 'But this is the life of a samurai. Come – we have work to do.'

CHAPTER 4

The attack

Autumn came. The leaves turned yellow and gold, and fell from the trees. Oishi sent messages to the ronin, and one by one they began to arrive in Edo. They travelled at different times, and went to different 'safe houses' in the city. Oishi made the journey in November 1702. When he arrived in Edo, he called a meeting in a room above a noisy restaurant.

'Now you must decide, for the last time,' he told his men. 'Do you want revenge for Lord Asano, or not? Some of you, I know, have young children, or very old parents. Do those men want to leave the league? You can go with honour.'

Eight men left. There were now forty-seven ronin in the league. There were young men and old men – the youngest was Chikara, now aged sixteen, and the oldest was seventy-six. There were brothers, and some fathers and sons, like Oishi and Chikara.

In the weeks before the attack, many of the ronin wrote letters home to their wives and families – to say their last goodbyes.

They began to get ready. One ronin had a ground plan of Kira's mansion, and Oishi studied this very carefully. There were high walls around the house – 132 metres on the long side and 61 metres on the short side. There were two gates, one in the east wall and one in the west wall. Inside the walls, there was a long building, with courtyards and gardens all around it.

'We need to go in at both gates at the same time,' said Oishi. 'We must have two groups of men, one to attack the front gate and one to attack the back gate.'

'Yes,' Yoshida said. 'And we must stop any servant from leaving the mansion. We don't want them to run across the river to the Uesugi and call for help.'

'How many people are living in Kira's mansion?' asked Hayami. 'And how many of them are samurai?'

There were high walls around the mansion.

'There are more than a hundred and twenty people inside those walls,' said Okuda. 'Perhaps about fifty of them are guards . . . We don't know how many samurai.'

'What about our weapons?' asked Oishi, looking at Horibe.

'The weapons are ready,' Horibe said. 'Everybody has their swords. We have spears for everybody too, and many bows and arrows. And we have armour.'

'Good,' said Oishi. 'So now we wait for the right time, when Kira is at home.'

The right time came on December 14, 1702, a dark night with snow falling from the sky. The people of Edo slept quietly, warm in their houses, but the ronin put on their armour, took their weapons, and waited for midnight.

Before they left, Oishi spoke to his men.

'At last we can finish our work for Lord Asano, and take revenge for his death, now nearly two years ago. We are here to kill Lord Kira Yoshinaka. We must fight his guards and his samurai, yes, and kill them, but do not kill women and children. We are not here to do that. And remember, you all have a whistle. When you find Lord Kira, blow your whistle.'

Then the forty-seven ronin went silently through the snow to Lord Kira's mansion. Oishi and Hara took their group to the front gate, and Yoshida with Oishi's son Chikara took their group of men to the back gate.

At the front gate, four men climbed over the wall.

Outside the mansion they put signs in the streets:
WE, THE RONIN FROM AKO CASTLE, ARE TAKING OUR
REVENGE ON KIRA YOSHINAKA TONIGHT, FOR THE DEATH
OF OUR *DAIMYO*, LORD ASANO NAGANORI. WE ARE NOT
NIGHT THIEVES AND DO NOT PLAN TO ATTACK OTHER
PEOPLE. YOU ARE SAFE IN YOUR HOUSES.

Later, when the neighbours came out into the streets,
they saw the signs, and went back into their houses.
They did not like Lord Kira, and so did nothing to
help him.

At the front gate, four men climbed over the wall,
and went silently into the guardroom. They fought the
guards and tied them up. Then they broke down the gate
from the inside, and Oishi and his men came into the
courtyard. At the same time, at the back gate, Yoshida

and Chikara and their men climbed over the wall into
the back courtyard. They tied up the guards there; then
waited quietly in the snow.

Before the attack began, Oishi sent four men up onto
the walls with bows and arrows. The great mansion was
still dark and silent, and Oishi whispered his orders.

'Lord Kira's servants are going to try and run away
to get help,' he said. 'Watch carefully, and shoot them
down at once. Nobody must leave!'

Now everything was ready, and Oishi beat his drum
loudly. The sound of the drum told the men at both
gates to start the attack at the same moment. The ronin
ran through the courtyards and gardens, and broke into
the house at the front and the back.

By now, everybody in the mansion was awake, and
Lord Kira's men, still in their nightclothes, came running

Oishi beat his drum loudly.

with swords and spears and knives. Suddenly, the night was full of noise – men shouting, the sound of sword against sword, the cries of women and children . . .

In the great front room of the mansion, the fighting was very fierce. Three of Kira's samurai, all famous swordsmen, fought for a long time, and Oishi's men could not get past them into the rooms behind. But the ronin fought hard too, and in the end Hara and two other ronin killed the three samurai. Then Oishi's men moved on into the next rooms.

At the other end of the long mansion, the fighting was also fierce. One of Kira's samurai attacked Yoshida, and jumped in under Yoshida's sword arm with his knife. Yoshida fell back, but Horibe was right behind the samurai, and cut him down with his long sword. Then the two ronin moved on into the next room.

Soon there was fighting in every room. Lord Kira's men fought bravely, but the ronin were fierce and deadly. Many men died, and some were hurt, but not one of the ronin died that night.

In every room Oishi and his men looked for Lord Kira, but he was never there. At last the two groups of ronin met in the middle of the mansion, and the fighting came to a stop. Seventeen of Kira's guards and samurai were dead, and the others ran away. Women and children sat in the corners of rooms, crying.

Oishi called out to Yoshida, 'Kira? Where is he?'

The fighting was very fierce.

'I don't know,' called Yoshida. 'He wasn't in the rooms at the back of the house when we came through.'

'What about the family living rooms?' called Horibe. 'Let's look in there again.'

'We can't lose Kira now!' shouted Okuda. 'Come on!'

The ronin began to feel afraid. *Where was Lord Kira? Was he still in the mansion somewhere? Or did he escape when the fighting began?* They ran through the family rooms, looking everywhere. In Kira's sleeping-room Oishi put his hand on the bed-clothes.

'They're warm!' he shouted. 'The bed-clothes are still warm – he was here not long ago! Find him!'

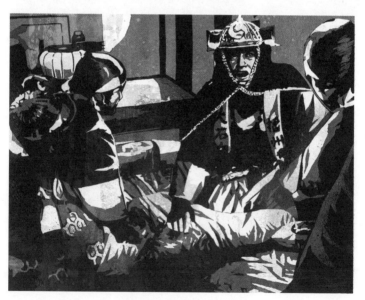

'The bed-clothes are still warm!' shouted Oishi.

CHAPTER 5

The revenge

Oishi sent his men, in four groups, to look everywhere – in the house, the kitchens, the gardens, the courtyards, the guardrooms, under the floors . . .

In the courtyard by the north wall, three of the ronin found a wood store. One of them, Hazama, went inside, and pushed his spear deep into the wood. There was a sudden cry, from under the wood. Immediately, the three ronin began to pull the wood out, and very quickly they found an old man, dressed in white nightclothes.

The three ronin began to pull the wood out.

'Old man, what is your name?' said Hazama.

The old man said nothing. He sat on the snowy ground, with his hands over his face.

'It's him,' said one of the ronin. 'Quick – blow your whistle.'

When they heard the whistle, all the ronin came running, with Oishi at the front.

Oishi carried a light, and held it near the old man's face. 'Yes, it's Kira,' he said to his men. 'See – here, on his head, that old cut. It was a cut made by a sword . . . Lord Asano's sword. It's in the right place.'

Oishi stood up, and bowed deeply to the old man.

'Lord Kira Yoshinaka, we are the samurai of Asano Naganori. We are loyal men, loyal to our master, and so we are here tonight to take revenge for his death. Lord Asano committed *seppuku*, and so we ask you, Lord Kira, to commit *seppuku* too – to die bravely, with honour.'

On the ground in front of Kira, Oishi carefully placed a long knife.

'Here, Lord Kira, is a knife. Lord Asano's knife.'

But the old man did nothing. He sat on the ground, shaking from head to toe, not speaking. Again and again, Oishi asked him to commit *seppuku*. Again and again, he showed him Lord Asano's knife. But Lord Kira did not move or put out his hand to take the knife. He did not want to take the road to death with honour.

At last, Oishi Yoshio stood up. He bowed again to

On the ground in front of Kira, Oishi carefully placed a long knife.

Lord Kira; then he drew his sword and cut off Lord Kira's head. The ronin put a coat around the head and tied it to a spear. It was three o'clock in the morning, and their long wait for revenge was finished.

'And now,' said Oishi, 'we must leave at once and take the head to Lord Asano's grave at Sengaku-ji. We must do this last thing for Lord Asano, and then we are ready for death.

'But before we leave,' he said, 'we must put out the house fires. We don't want to start a fire in the city.' The house was full of dead bodies and crying women, and there was no one to take care of things. Edo was a city of buildings made of wood, and fire was a terrible danger.

They put out the fires, and forty-six ronin left the mansion. The forty-seventh ronin, a young man called Terasaka, was now on his way to Hiroshima. Oishi sent him there to take the news of the attack to Daigaku, the brother of Lord Asano.

Two of the ronin carried the spear with Lord Kira's head, and Oishi walked in front, with Yoshida on one side and Chikara on the other side.

They began their long walk to Sengaku-ji. And in the streets of Edo, people came out of their houses to watch.

CHAPTER 6

The punishment

The Asano family graves were next to the temple at Sengaku-ji, and it was a ten-kilometre walk there from Kira's mansion. The ronin were afraid of attack from the Uesugi guards, so they kept away from Edo Palace and walked on the eastern side of the Sumida River until the Eitai bridge. Then they crossed the river. Oishi sent two of the ronin to Edo Palace, to take the news of the ronins' revenge to the government.

In the first light of day more and more people came out into the streets – talking and whispering about the killing of Lord Kira and the revenge of the forty-seven ronin. The news ran like fire through the city.

And the people liked the news. 'What brave men!' they said. 'What loyal samurai! These ronin waited nearly two years to take their revenge! That is the samurai code! They are true samurai, like in the old days.'

The ronin passed Zojo-ji temple, and began to climb the hill to Sengaku-ji. When they arrived at the temple, they washed Lord Kira's head in the well (you can see the well to this day at Sengaku-ji).

Then, slowly and carefully, Oishi placed the head in front of Lord Asano's grave. The forty-six ronin kneeled before the grave, and Oishi spoke these words: 'For many years, Lord Asano, we served you, we ate

your food, we lived in your castle. You tried to kill your
enemy, but you lost your life. We could not live under

The forty-six ronin kneeled before Lord Asano's grave.

the same sky as your enemy. Last night we finished your work, and took revenge for your death.

'Young and old, we, the ronin of Ako, are your loyal servants. We serve you, by sword and by spear, in life and in death.'

For two days Kira's head lay on Lord Asano's grave at Sengaku-ji. Then the temple priests took it away and sent it back to his family.

The Shogun's officers arrested the forty-six ronin and took them to the mansions of four different *daimyo*. There, the ronin waited to hear their punishment. Oishi, with sixteen of his men, went to the Hosokawa mansion near Sengaku-ji. To honour them, 1,400 samurai walked with them through the snowy streets, and the people of the city watched.

Now came a difficult time for the Shogun and the government. Killing was a crime, and in those days the punishment for that crime was to cut off the head. But a death like that was a death without honour.

Many people said this: 'The ronin are good samurai – brave men, loyal to their master. They were right to kill Kira and to take revenge for their lord's death. They followed the samurai code of honour, so they must have a samurai death.'

But other people thought differently, and said this: 'Lord Asano attacked Lord Kira in the palace, and Asano died because of this crime. Lord Kira did not kill him, so there was no need for revenge. This was not a revenge killing, and the ronin are just killers. So they must die a killer's death.'

The government could not agree on the punishment. For weeks they talked and argued, asked this person and that person, talked and argued again. The ronin waited quietly in the four *daimyo* houses. They waited for death, one way or another.

At last, one day in March 1703, many weeks after the death of Kira, the order came from the Shogun's palace. The ronin must die, but because of their loyalty to their lord, they could die the samurai death. They could commit *seppuku* and keep their honour as samurai.

That same day, in the four *daimyo* mansions, the ronin got ready for death. One by one, in the courtyards of the mansions, the forty-six ronin committed *seppuku*. Their bodies were put in graves at Sengaku-ji temple, close to their master, Lord Asano Naganori.

The forty-seventh ronin, Terasaka, arrived back from Hiroshima after the death of the other ronin. He went at once to Edo Palace, and asked for the same death as the other ronin. But he was a young man, and the Shogun felt sorry for him. So Terasaka did not commit *seppuku*. He lived to the great age of eighty-three, but when he died, he wanted to be with the other ronin. So his grave is the forty-seventh grave at Sengaku-ji.

The ronin got ready for death.

Sengaku-ji today

Three hundred years later, people in Japan are still talking and arguing about the story of the Forty-Seven Ronin. Every year, on December 14, there is a festival at the Sengaku-ji temple to remember Lord Asano's death and the revenge of his brave, loyal ronin. Thousands of people come every year to this festival. The way of the samurai is not forgotten.

GLOSSARY

argue to talk angrily with someone because you do not agree

armour metal 'clothes' to cover the body when fighting

arrest (*v & n*) to take a person away because of a crime

attack (*v & n*) to start fighting or hurting somebody or something

beat (**a drum**) to hit something very hard many times

blow (**a whistle**) to send air out from your mouth through a whistle (a small musical instrument)

bow and arrow a weapon made of wood and string which sends arrows (thin wooden sticks with sharp ends) through the air

bow (*v & n*) to bend your head or body forward to show respect

brave ready to do dangerous or difficult things without fear

captain the leader of a group of people

castle a large old building with high strong walls to keep people safe from attack

ceremony a formal public event when things are always done in the same special way (*adj* **ceremonial**)

code a set of rules for a group of people

commit to do (used with words like *suicide* (*seppuku*), *crime*, etc.)

courtyard an open space without a roof between buildings

crime something that somebody does that is against the law

daimyo *see page iv*

draw (**a sword**) to pull or take something from a place

drum a musical instrument that you hit with special sticks or with your hands

fierce angry and wild

gate a 'door' in a wall

government the group of people who control a country

grave (*n*) the place where a person's dead body is put

guard (*n*) a person who keeps somebody or something safe from
    attack by other people
honour knowing and doing what is right, which causes other
    people to respect you and think well of you
kneel to bend your legs and rest on your knees
league a group of people that work together to do something
lift (*v*) to move something to a higher place
lord a title for a man who has an important position in society
loyal staying true and faithful to someone (*n* **loyalty**)
mansion a very big, grand house
master a man who is the leader, or lord, of other people
message words that one person sends to another
officer a person who gives orders to other people
order (*n*) words that tell somebody to do something
palace a very large, beautiful house for a king, emperor, etc.
powerful strong, able to do many things, control people, etc.
present (*n*) something that you give to somebody
price how much money you pay to buy something
priest a person who leads people in their religion
punishment something that is done to a person because they
    have done something wrong
revenge something bad that you do to somebody who has done
    something bad to you
ronin *see page iv*
ruler a person who rules a country (e.g. a queen, an emperor,
    a president, etc.)
samurai *see page iv*
seppuku *see page iv*
servant somebody who works in another person's house
serve to do work for other people
Shogun *see page iv*
spear a long stick, sharp at one end, used for fighting

spy   a person who tries to learn secrets about an enemy

sword   a weapon that looks like a very long sharp knife

take care of   to do everything that is necessary for something or somebody

temple   a building where people go to talk to a god or gods

tie (*v*)   to fix something using rope, string, etc.

tie (somebody) up   to put a piece of rope around somebody because you don't want them to move or escape

warrior   a person (in the past) who fights in a battle or war

weapon   something that is used for fighting or killing people

well (*n*)   a deep hole for getting water from under the ground

whisper   to speak very quietly in a soft voice

whistle (*n*)   a small musical instrument that makes a long high sound when you blow it

wood store   a place to keep wood for a fire

ACTIVITIES

Before Reading

1 **Read the back cover of the book, and the introduction on the first page. How much do you know now about the story? Tick one box for each sentence.**

YES NO

1 The story of the forty-seven ronin happened
  3,000 years ago. ☐ ☐
2 It is a story about revenge. ☐ ☐
3 One day in 1701 Lord Kira dies. ☐ ☐
4 When a lord dies, his samurai become ronin. ☐ ☐
5 Ronin are samurai without a lord or master. ☐ ☐
6 People in Japan still remember this story today. ☐ ☐

2 **What is going to happen in this story? Can you guess? Choose one answer for each question.**

1 What do the ronin use for fighting?
  a) Their hands.   b) Swords.   c) Guns.
2 How long does the plan for revenge take?
  a) Two years.   b) Five years.   c) Ten years.
3 What revenge do the ronin want? Do they want Lord Kira . . .
  a) to leave Japan?   b) to die?   c) to pay them money?
4 The story begins with a death. Is it going to end with . . .
  a) one death?   b) two deaths?   c) many deaths?

ACTIVITIES

While Reading

Read chapters 1 to 3, and then complete these sentences with the right words.

ceremony, crime, loyal, revenge, spy

1 Lord Kira was the teacher of _____ at the palace.
2 It was a _____ to draw a sword in the Shogun's palace.
3 It was the samurai way to take _____ for a lord's death.
4 The ronin were _____ to their lord in life and in death.
5 The cook in Oishi's house was a _____ for Lord Kira.

Read chapters 4 and 5. Read these short extracts, and answer the questions.

1 *'We must stop any servant from leaving the mansion.'* (page 26) Why was it important to do that?
2 *'The bed-clothes are still warm.'* (page 32) What did this mean?
3 *On the ground in front of Kira, Oishi carefully placed a long knife.* (page 34) Why did Oishi do this?

Before you read chapter 6, can you guess what happens?

1 All the ronin die.
2 Forty-six ronin die.
3 The ronin do not die; they go to prison.

ACTIVITIES

After Reading

1 **Match these parts of sentences together, and choose the best linking word to join them.**

1 Lord Asano was angry with Lord Kira . . .

2 He drew a sword and attacked Kira, . . .

3 The punishment for this crime was death, . . .

4 Lord Asano's samurai were now ronin, . . .

5 They planned to attack Lord Kira and kill him, . . .

6 Lord Kira was afraid of an attack by Asano's ronin, . . .

7 On the night of the attack Oishi and his men looked for Lord Kira everywhere in the mansion, . . .

8 Lord Kira did not want to commit *seppuku*, . . .

9 The ronin carried Kira's head on a spear to Sengaku-ji . . .

10 *when* / *and* they wanted revenge for their lord's death.

11 *and* / *but* at last they found him in the wood store.

12 *because* /*so* Lord Asano committed *seppuku*.

13 *but* / *and* it was two years before they could attack.

14 *because* / *so* Kira called him 'stupid' and 'slow'.

15 *so* / *but* he put many Uesugi guards around his mansion.

16 *and* / *but* placed the head in front of Lord Asano's grave.

17 *because* / *so* Oishi cut off his head with a sword.

18 *and* / *but* it was a crime to draw a sword inside the palace.

2 **Here is a conversation between Hara and Kataoka, when Hara visits Oishi in Kyoto. Put their conversation in the right order, and write in the speakers' names. Hara speaks first (number 3).**

1 _____ 'He sees a samurai without honour.'

2 _____ 'This happens – when Kira is no longer afraid of us ronin, what's he going to do?'

3 _Hara_ 'Why is Oishi spending all his time in the town with all kinds of bad men?'

4 _____ 'It's clever because it's hiding something. Think about it, Hara. What do we ronin all want?'

5 _____ 'Clever? What do you mean, 'clever'? How is that clever, Kataoka?'

6 _____ 'Right again! And then, when there's only a small number of guards round his mansion, we can . . .'

7 _____ 'Nobody. Ah! I begin to understand! So what happens next, Kataoka?'

8 _____ 'Because he's clever.'

9 _____ 'We want revenge on Lord Kira, of course. We're going to attack his mansion, find him, and kill him.'

10 _____ 'Right, Hara! And who is afraid of a samurai without honour?'

11 _____ '. . . attack! You're right, Kataoka – it is clever!'

12 _____ 'Yes, we are. And Lord Kira knows that. So he's watching Oishi, our captain. And what does Kira see?'

13 _____ 'He's going to send the Uesugi guards home.'

3 Complete this crossword with words from the story. Use the clues below to help you.

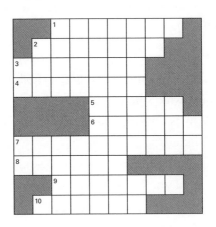

1 Oishi was the _____ of the ronin.

2 In old Japan, the _____ were famous fighting men.

3 The ronin wanted _____ for Lord Asano's death.

4 A samurai was a _____, a fighting man, and he served one of the great Japanese lords.

5 The favourite weapon of the samurai was the _____.

6 For a samurai, it was better to die than to live a life without _____.

7 In the Shogun's palace Lord Asano wore special _____ clothes.

8 Ronin were samurai without a lord or _____.

9 Lord Kira lived in a _____, a very big, grand house.

10 Oishi was at home in Ako _____ on the day when Lord Asano died.

4 Look back at the crossword and find a hidden word of ten letters. What is it?

The hidden word is _____.

5 The hidden word from the crossword can mean different things to different people at different times. Talk about your answers to these questions.

1 In Japan in 1702, after Lord Kira's death, what did this word mean to the ronin?

2 In today's world, what can this word mean to . . .
   a) a murderer?
   b) a thief?
   c) a child in school?
   d) somebody parking their car in the wrong place?

6 What did you think about the people in this story? Choose some names, and finish the sentences in your own words.

Lord Kira / Lord Asano / Oishi / Riku / Chikara

1 I felt sorry for _____ because _____.
2 I liked _____ because _____.
3 I didn't like _____ because _____.
4 I was angry with _____ when _____.
5 I was afraid for _____ when _____.
6 _____ was right to _____.
7 _____ was wrong to _____.

ABOUT THE AUTHOR

Jennifer Bassett has worked in English Language Teaching since 1972. She has been a teacher, teacher trainer, editor, and materials writer, and has taught in England, Greece, Spain, and Portugal. She is the Series Editor of the *Oxford Bookworms Library*, and has written nearly forty original and retold graded readers. Her Bookworms titles include *The Phantom of the Opera*, *One-Way Ticket*, *The President's Murderer*, *The Omega Files*, *Shirley Homes and the Lithuanian Case*, *Shirley Homes and the Cyber Thief*, *Les Misérables*, all at Stage 1, and *William Shakespeare* at Stage 2.

Three of her adaptations, *Rabbit-Proof Fence* (Stage 3), *Love Among the Haystacks* (Stage 2), and Les Misérables (Stage 1), have won Language Learner Literature Awards from the Extensive Reading Foundation <www.erfoundation.com>, and five of her other titles have been finalists for the Awards. She has also created a new sub-series called *Bookworms World Stories*, which are collections of short stories written in English from around the world. With H. G. Widdowson, she is series co-adviser of the *Oxford Bookworms Collection*, volumes of unadapted short stories for advanced learners.

Jennifer lives and works in Devonshire, in south-west England. She loves travelling and has visited Japan several times. On one of her visits she saw the temple at Sengaku-ji, and this began her interest in the famous story of the forty-seven ronin.

OXFORD BOOKWORMS LIBRARY

Classics • Crime & Mystery • Factfiles • Fantasy & Horror
Human Interest • Playscripts • Thriller & Adventure
True Stories • World Stories

The OXFORD BOOKWORMS LIBRARY provides enjoyable reading in English, with a wide range of classic and modern fiction, non-fiction, and plays. It includes original and adapted texts in seven carefully graded language stages, which take learners from beginner to advanced level. An overview is given on the next pages.

All Stage 1 titles are available as audio recordings, as well as over eighty other titles from Starter to Stage 6. All Starters and many titles at Stages 1 to 4 are specially recommended for younger learners. Every Bookworm is illustrated, and Starters and Factfiles have full-colour illustrations.

The OXFORD BOOKWORMS LIBRARY also offers extensive support. Each book contains an introduction to the story, notes about the author, a glossary, and activities. Additional resources include tests and worksheets, and answers for these and for the activities in the books. There is advice on running a class library, using audio recordings, and the many ways of using Oxford Bookworms in reading programmes. Resource materials are available on the website <www.oup.com/elt/gradedreaders>.

The *Oxford Bookworms Collection* is a series for advanced learners. It consists of volumes of short stories by well-known authors, both classic and modern. Texts are not abridged or adapted in any way, but carefully selected to be accessible to the advanced student.

You can find details and a full list of titles in the *Oxford Bookworms Library Catalogue* and *Oxford English Language Teaching Catalogues*, and on the website <www.oup.com/elt/gradedreaders>.

THE OXFORD BOOKWORMS LIBRARY
GRADING AND SAMPLE EXTRACTS

STARTER • 250 HEADWORDS

present simple – present continuous – imperative –
can/cannot, must – going to (future) – simple gerunds …

Her phone is ringing – but where is it?

Sally gets out of bed and looks in her bag. No phone. She looks under the bed. No phone. Then she looks behind the door. There is her phone. Sally picks up her phone and answers it. *Sally's Phone*

STAGE 1 • 400 HEADWORDS

… past simple – coordination with *and*, *but*, *or* –
subordination with *before*, *after*, *when*, *because*, *so* …

I knew him in Persia. He was a famous builder and I worked with him there. For a time I was his friend, but not for long. When he came to Paris, I came after him – I wanted to watch him. He was a very clever, very dangerous man. *The Phantom of the Opera*

STAGE 2 • 700 HEADWORDS

… present perfect – *will* (future) – (*don't*) *have to*, *must not*, *could* –
comparison of adjectives – simple *if* clauses – past continuous –
tag questions – *ask/tell* + infinitive …

While I was writing these words in my diary, I decided what to do. I must try to escape. I shall try to get down the wall outside. The window is high above the ground, but I have to try. I shall take some of the gold with me – if I escape, perhaps it will be helpful later. *Dracula*

STAGE 3 • 1000 HEADWORDS

… should, may – present perfect continuous – *used to* – past perfect –
causative – relative clauses – indirect statements …

Of course, it was most important that no one should see
Colin, Mary, or Dickon entering the secret garden. So Colin
gave orders to the gardeners that they must all keep away
from that part of the garden in future. *The Secret Garden*

STAGE 4 • 1400 HEADWORDS

… past perfect continuous – passive (simple forms) –
would conditional clauses – indirect questions –
relatives with *where/when* – gerunds after prepositions/phrases …

I was glad. Now Hyde could not show his face to the world
again. If he did, every honest man in London would be proud
to report him to the police. *Dr Jekyll and Mr Hyde*

STAGE 5 • 1800 HEADWORDS

… future continuous – future perfect –
passive (modals, continuous forms) –
would have conditional clauses – modals + perfect infinitive …

If he had spoken Estella's name, I would have hit him. I was so
angry with him, and so depressed about my future, that I could
not eat the breakfast. Instead I went straight to the old house.
Great Expectations

STAGE 6 • 2500 HEADWORDS

… passive (infinitives, gerunds) – advanced modal meanings –
clauses of concession, condition

When I stepped up to the piano, I was confident. It was as if I
knew that the prodigy side of me really did exist. And when I
started to play, I was so caught up in how lovely I looked that
I didn't worry how I would sound. *The Joy Luck Club*

BOOKWORMS • TRUE STORIES • STAGE 1

Mutiny on the Bounty

TIM VICARY

It is night in the south seas near Tahiti, and the ship *HMS Bounty* has begun the long voyage home to England. But the sailors on the ship are angry men, and they have swords and guns. They pull the captain out of bed and take him up on deck. He tries to run, but a sailor holds a knife to his neck. 'Do that again, Captain Bligh, and you're a dead man!' he says.

The mutiny on the Bounty happened in April, 1789. This is the true story of Captain Bligh and Fletcher Christian, and the ship that never came home to England.

BOOKWORMS • TRUE STORIES • STAGE 1

Ned Kelly: A True Story

CHRISTINE LINDOP

When he was a boy, he was poor and hungry. When he was a young man, he was still poor and hungry. He learnt how to steal horses, he learnt how to fight, he learnt how to live – outside the law. Australia in the 1870s was a hard, wild place. Rich people had land, poor people didn't. So the rich got richer, and the poor stayed poor.

Some say Ned Kelly was a bad man. Some say he was a good man but the law was bad. This is the true story of Australia's most famous outlaw.